Tertullian

On Repentance

Tertullian

On Repentance

Tertullian
On Repentance

Published by
Lighthouse Christian Publishing
SAN 257-4330
5531 Dufferin Drive
Savage, Minnesota, 55378
United States of America

www.lighthousechristianpublishing.com

Tertullian

Introductory Note.

The Second Class of Tertullian's works, according to the logical method I have endeavored to carry out, is that which includes his treatises against the heresies of his times. In these, the genius of our author is brilliantly illustrated, while, in melancholy fact, he is demonstrating the folly of his own final lapse and the wickedness of that schism and heresy into which he fell away from Truth. Were it not that history abounds in like examples of the frailty of the human intellect and of the insufficiency of "man that walketh to direct his steps," we should be forced to a theory of mental decay to account for inconsistencies so gross and for delusions so besotted. "Genius to madness is *indeed* allied," and who knows but something like that imbecility which closed the career of Swift may have been the fate of this splendid wit and versatile man of parts? Charity, admiration and love force this inquiry upon my own mind continually, as I explore his fascinating pages. And the order in which the student will find them in this series, will lead, I think, to similar reflections on the part of many readers. We observe a natural bent and turn of mind, even in his Catholic writings, which indicate his perils. These are more and more apparent in his recent works, as his enthusiasm heats itself into a frenzy which at last becomes a rage. He breaks down by degrees, as in orthodoxy so also in force and in character. It is almost like the collapse of Solomon or of Bacon. And though our own times have produced no example of stars of equal magnitude, to become falling-stars, we have seen illustrations the most humiliating, of those calm words of Bishop Kaye: "Human nature often presents the curious phenomenon of a union of the most opposite qualities in the same mind; of vigor, acuteness and discrimination on some subjects, with imbecility, dullness and bigotry on others." Milton, himself another example of his own threnode, breaks forth in this splendid utterance of lyrical confession:

> "God of our fathers what is man?
> Nor do I name of men the common rout,
> That, wandering loose about,
> Grow up and perish as the summer fly,
> Heads without name, no more remembered,
> But such as thou hast solemnly elected,
> With gifts and graces eminently adorned,
> To some great work, thy glory
> And people's safety, *which in part they effect*."

And here, I must venture a remark on the ambiguity of the expressions concerning our author's Montanism. In the treatise against Marcion, written late in his career, Tertullian identifies himself with the Church and strenuously defends its faith and its apostolic order. In only rare instances does his weakness for the "new prophecy" crop out, and then, it is only as one identifies himself with a school within the church. Precisely so Fenelon maintained his milder Montanism, without a thought of deserting the Latin Church. Afterwards Fenelon drew back, but at last poor Tertullian fell away. So with the Jansenists. They credited the *miracles* and the *convulsions* (or ecstasies) of their school, and condemned those who rejected them, as Tertullian condemns the *Psychics*. The great expounder of the Nicene Faith (Bp. Bull) does indeed speak very decidedly of Tertullian as a *lapser*, even when he wrote his first book against Marcion. His semi-schismatic position must be allowed. But, was it a *formal* lapse at that time? The English non-jurors were long in communion with the Church, even while they denounced their brethren and the "Erastianizing" clergy, much as Tertullian does the *Psychics*. St. Augustine speaks of *Tertullianists* with great moderation, and notes the final downfall of our author as something distinct from Tertullianism. When we reflect, therefore, that only four of all his varied writings (now extant) are proofs of an accomplished lapse, ought we not carefully to maintain the distinction between the Montanistic Tertullian and Tertullian the Montanist? Bishop Bull, it seems to me would not object to this way of putting it, when we consider his own discrimination in the following weighty words. He says:

"A clear distinction must be made between those works which Tertullian, when already a Montanist, wrote specifically in defense of Montanism *against the church*, and those which he composed, as a Montanist indeed, yet *not in defense of Montanism against the church*, but rather, *in defense of the common doctrines of the church*—and of Montanus, in opposition to other heretics."

Now in arranging the works of this second class, *the Prescription* comes logically first, because, written in Orthodoxy, it forcibly upholds the Scriptural Rule of Faith, the Catholic touchstone of all professed verity. It is also a necessary Introduction to the great work against Marcion which I have placed next in order; giving it the precedence to which it is entitled in part on chronological ground, in part because of the general purity of its material with the exhibition it presents of the author's mental processes and of his very gradual decline from Truth.

Very fortunate were the Edinburgh Editors in securing for this work and some others, the valuable labors of Dr. Holmes, of whom I have elsewhere given some biographical particulars. The merit and fullness of his annotations are so marked, that I have been spared a great deal of work, such as I was forced to bestow on the former volumes of this American Edition. But on the other hand these pages have given me much patient study and toil as an editor, because of the "shreds and patches" in which Tertullian comes to us, in the Edinburgh Series; and because of some typographical peculiarities, exceptional in that Series itself, and presenting complications, when transferred to a new form of mechanical arrangement. For example, apart from some valuable material which belongs to the General Preface, and which I have transferred accordingly, the following dislocations confronted me to begin with: The *Marcion* is presented to us in Volume VII. apart from the other writings of Tertullian. At the close of Vol. XI. we reach the *Ad Nationes*, of which Dr. Holmes is the translator, another hand (Mr. Thelwall's) having been employed on former pages of that volume. It is not till we reach Volume XV. that Tertullian again appears, but this volume is wholly the work of Dr. Holmes. Finally, in Volume XVIII., we meet Tertullian again, (Mr. Thelwall the able translator), but, here is placed the "Introduction" to all the works of Tertullian, which, of course, I have, transferred to its proper place. I make these explanations by no means censoriously, but to point out at once the nature of my own task, and the advantage that accrues to the reader, by the order in which the works of the great Tertullian appear in this edition, enabling him to compare different or parallel passages, all methodically arranged in consecutive pages, without a minute's search, or delay.

Now, as to typographical difficulties to which I have referred, Dr. Holmes marks all his multiplied and useful notes with *brackets*, which are almost always superfluous, and which in this American Edition are used to designate my own contributions, when printed with the text, or apart from Preface and Elucidations. These, therefore, I have removed necessarily and with no appreciable loss to the work, but great gain to the beauty of the page. But, again, Dr. Holmes' translations are all so heavily bracketed as to become an eyesore, and the disfigured pages have been often complained of as afflictive to the reader. Many words strictly implied by the original Latin, and which should therefore be unmarked, are yet put between brackets. Even minute words (*and*, or *to wit*, or *again*,) when, in the nature of the case the English idiom requires them, are thus marked. I have not retained these blemishes; but when an inconsiderable word or a repetition does add to the sense, or qualify it, I have italicized such words, throwing more important interpolations into parenthetical marks, which are less painful to the sight than brackets. I have found them quite as serviceable to denote the auxiliary word or phrase; and where the author himself uses a parenthesis, I have observed very few instances in which a sensible reader would confound it with the translator's efforts to eke out the sense. Sometimes, an awkward interpolation has been thrown into a footnote.

Occasionally the crabbed sentences of the great Carthaginian are so obscure that Dr. Holmes has been unable to make them lucid, although, with the original in hand, he probably felt a force in his own rendering which the mere English reader must fail to perceive. In a few such instances, noting the fact in the margin, I have tried to bring out the sense, by slight modifications of punctuation and arrangement. Occasionally too I have dropped a superfluous interpolation (such as *e.g.*, *to conclude*, or let me say again,) when I have found that it only served to clog and overcharge a sentence. Last of all, Dr. Holmes' *headings* have sometimes been condensed, to avoid phrases and sentences immediately recurring in the chapter. These purely mechanical parts require a terse form of statement, like those in the English Bible, and I have frequently reduced them on that model, dropping redundant adverbs and adjectives to bring out the catchwords.

On Repentance.

Chapter I.—Of Heathen Repentance.

Repentance, men understand, so far as nature is able, to be an emotion of the mind arising from disgust at some previously cherished worse sentiment: that kind of men I mean which even we ourselves were in days gone by—blind, without the Lord's light. From the reason of repentance, however, they are just as far as they are from the Author of reason Himself. Reason, in fact, is a thing of God, inasmuch as there is nothing which God the Maker of all has not provided, disposed, ordained by reason—nothing which He has not willed should be handled and understood by reason. All, therefore, who are ignorant of God, must necessarily be ignorant also of a thing which is His, because no treasure-house at all is accessible to strangers. And thus, voyaging all the universal course of life without the rudder of reason, they know not how to shun the hurricane which is impending over the world. Moreover, how irrationally they behave in the practice of repentance, it will be enough briefly to show just by this one fact, that they exercise it even in the case of their good deeds. They repent of good faith, of love, of simple-heartedness, of patience, of mercy, just in proportion as any deed prompted by these feelings has fallen on thankless soil. They execrate their own selves for having done good; and that species chiefly of repentance which is applied to the best works they fix in their heart, making it their care to remember never again to do a good turn. On repentance for evil deeds, on the contrary, they lay lighter stress. In short, they make this same (virtue) a means of sinning more readily than a means of right doing.

Chapter II—True Repentance a Thing Divine, Originated by God, and Subject to His Laws.

But if they acted as men who had any part in God, and thereby in reason also, they would first weigh well the importance of repentance, and would never apply it in such a way as to make it a ground for convicting themselves of perverse self-amendment. In short, they would regulate the limit of their repentance, because they would reach (a limit) in sinning too—by fearing God, I mean. But where there is no fear, in like manner there is no amendment; where there is no amendment, repentance is of necessity vain, for it lacks the fruit for which God sowed it; that is, man's salvation. For God—after so many and so great sins of human temerity, begun by the first of the race, Adam, after the condemnation of man, together with the dowry of the world after his ejection from paradise and subjection to death—when He had hasted back to His own mercy, did from that time onward inaugurate repentance in His own self, by rescinding the sentence of His first wrath, engaging to grant pardon to His own work and image. And so He gathered together a people for Himself, and fostered them with many liberal distributions of His bounty, and, after so often finding them most ungrateful, ever exhorted them to repentance and sent out the voices of the universal company of the prophets to prophesy. By and by, promising freely the grace which in the last times He was intending to pour as a flood of light on the universal world through His Spirit, He bade the baptism of repentance lead the way, with the view of first preparing, by means of the sign and seal of repentance, them whom He was calling, through grace, to (inherit) the promise surely made to Abraham. John holds not his peace, saying, "Enter upon repentance, for now shall salvation approach the nations"—the Lord, that is, bringing salvation according to God's promise. To Him John, as His harbinger, directed the repentance (which he preached), whose province was the purging of men's minds, that whatever defilement inveterate error had imparted, whatever contamination in the heart of man ignorance had engendered, that repentance should sweep and scrape away, and cast out of doors, and thus prepare the home of the heart, by making it clean, for the Holy Spirit, who was about to supervene, that He might with pleasure introduce Himself there-into, together with His celestial blessings. Of these blessings the title is briefly one—the salvation of man—the abolition of former sins being the preliminary step. This is the (final) cause of repentance, this her work, in taking in hand the business of divine mercy. What is profitable to man does service to God. The rule of repentance, however, which we learn when we know the Lord, retains a definite form—viz., that no violent hands so to speak, be ever laid on good deeds or thoughts. For God, never giving His sanction to the reprobation of good deeds, inasmuch as they are His own (of which, being the author, He must necessarily be the defender too), is in like manner the acceptor of them, and if the acceptor, likewise the rewarder. Let, then, the ingratitude of men see to it, if it attaches repentance even to good works; let their gratitude see to it too, if the desire of earning it be the incentive to well-doing: earthly and mortal are they each. For how small is your gain if you do good to a grateful man! or your loss if to an ungrateful! A good deed has God as its debtor, just as an evil has too; for a judge is rewarder of every cause. Well, since, God as Judge presides over the exacting and maintaining of justice, which to Him is most dear; and since it is with an eye to justice that He appoints all the sum of His discipline, is there room for doubting that, just as in all our acts universally, so also in the case of repentance, justice must be rendered to God?—which duty can indeed only be fulfilled on the condition that repentance be brought to bear only on sins. Further, no deed but an evil one deserves to be called sin, nor does anyone err by well-doing. But if he does not err, why does he invade (the province of) repentance, the private ground of such as do err? Why does he impose on his goodness a duty proper to wickedness? Thus it comes to pass that, when a thing is called into play where it ought not, there, where it ought, it is neglected.

Chapter III—Sins May Be Divided into Corporeal and Spiritual. Both Equally Subject, If Not to Human, Yet to Divine Investigation and Punishment.

What things, then, they be for which repentance seems just and due—that is, what things are to be set down under the head of sin—the occasion indeed demands that I should note down; but (to do so) may seem to be unnecessary. For when the Lord is known, our spirit, having been "looked back upon" by its own Author, emerges unbidden into the knowledge of the truth; and being admitted to (an acquaintance with) the divine precepts, is by them forthwith instructed that "that from which God bids us abstain is to be accounted sin:" inasmuch as, since it is generally agreed that God is some great essence of good, of course nothing but evil would be displeasing to good; in that, between things mutually contrary, friendship there is none. Still it will not be irksome briefly to touch upon the fact that, of sins, some are carnal, that is, corporeal; some spiritual. For since man is composed of this combination of a two-fold substance, the sources of his sins are no other than the sources of his composition. But it is not the fact that body and spirit are two things that constitute the sins mutually different—otherwise they are on this account rather equal, because the two make up one—lest any make the distinction between their sins proportionate to the difference between their substances, so as to esteem the one lighter, or else heavier, than the other: if it be true, (as it is,) that both flesh and spirit are creatures of God; one wrought by His hand, one consummated by His afflatus. Since, then, they equally pertain to the Lord, whichever of them sins equally offends the Lord. Is it for you to distinguish the acts of the flesh and the spirit, whose communion and conjunction in life, in death, and in resurrection, are so intimate, that "at that time" they are equally raised up either for life or else for judgment; because, to wit, they have equally either sinned or lived innocently? This we would (once for all) premise, in order that we may understand that no less necessity for repentance is incumbent on either part of man, if in anything it have sinned, than on both. The guilt of both is common; common, too, is the Judge—God to wit; common, therefore, is withal the healing medicine of repentance. The source whence sins are named "spiritual" and "corporeal" is the fact that every sin is matter either of actor else of thought: so that what is indeed is "corporeal," because a deed, like a body, is capable of being seen and touched; what is in the mind is "spiritual," because spirit is neither seen nor handled: by which consideration is shown that sins not of deed only, but of will too, are to be shunned, and by repentance purged. For if human finitude judges only sins of deed, because it is not equal to (piercing) the lurking-places of the will, let us not on that account make light of crimes of the will in God's sight. God is all-sufficient. Nothing from whence any sin whatsoever proceeds is remote from His sight; because He is neither ignorant, nor does He omit to decree it to judgment. He is no dissembler of, nor double-dealer with, His own clear-sightedness. What (shall we say of the fact) that will is the origin of deed? For if any sins are imputed to chance, or to necessity, or to ignorance, let them see to themselves: if these be excepted, there is no sinning save by will. Since, then, will is the origin of deed, is it not so much the rather amenable to penalty as it is first in guilt? Nor, if some difficulty interferes with its full accomplishment, is it even in that case exonerated; for it is itself imputed to itself: nor; having done the work which lay in its own power, will it be excusable by reason of that miscarriage of its accomplishment. In fact, how does the Lord demonstrate Himself as adding a superstructure to the Law, except by interdicting sins of the will as well (as other sins); while He defines not only the man who had actually invaded another's wedlock to be an adulterer, but likewise him who had contaminated (a woman) by the concupiscence of his gaze? Accordingly, it is dangerous enough for the mind to set before itself what it is forbidden to perform, and rashly through the will to perfect its execution. And since the power of this will is such that, even without fully sating its self-gratification, it stands for a deed; as a deed, therefore, it shall be punished. It is utterly vain to say, "I willed, but yet I did not." Rather you ought to carry the thing through, because you will; or else not to will, because you do not carry it through. But, by the confession of your consciousness, you pronounce your own condemnation. For if you eagerly desired a good thing, you would have been anxious to carry it through; in like manner, as you do not carry an evil thing through, you ought not to have eagerly desired it. Wherever you take your stand, you are fast bound by guilt; because you have either willed evil, or else have not fulfilled good.

Chapter IV. —Repentance Applicable to All the Kinds of Sin. To Be Practiced Not Only, Nor Chiefly, for the Good It Brings, But Because God Commands It.

To all sins, then, committed whether by flesh or spirit, whether by deed or will, the same God who has destined penalty by means of judgment, has withal engaged to grant pardon by means of repentance, saying to the people, "Repent thee, and I will save thee;" and again, "I live, saith the Lord, and I will (have) repentance rather than death." Repentance, then, is "life," since it is preferred to "death." That repentance, O sinner, like myself (nay, rather, less than myself, for pre-eminence in sins I acknowledge to be mine), do you so hasten to, so embrace, as a shipwrecked man the protection of some plank. This will draw you forth when sunk in the waves of sins, and will bear you forward into the port of the divine clemency. Seize the opportunity of unexpected felicity: that you, who sometime were in God's sight nothing but "a drop of a bucket," and "dust of the threshing floor," and "a potter's vessel," may thenceforward become that "tree which is sown beside the waters, is perennial in leaves, bears fruit at its own time," and shall not see "fire," nor "axe." Having found "the truth," repent of errors; repent of having loved what God loves not: even we ourselves do not permit our slave-lads not to hate the things which are offensive to us; for the principle of voluntary obedience consists in similarity of minds.

To reckon up the good, of repentance, the subject-matter is copious, and therefore should be committed to great eloquence. Let us, however, in proportion to our narrow abilities, inculcate one point—that what God enjoins is good and best. I hold it audacity to dispute about the "good" of a divine precept; for, indeed, it is not the fact that it is good which binds us to obey, but the fact that God has enjoined it. To exact the rendering of obedience the majesty of divine power has the prior right; the authority of Him who commands is prior to the utility of him who serves. "Is it good to repent, or no?" Why do you ponder? God enjoins; nay, He not merely enjoins, but likewise exhorts. He invites by (offering) reward—salvation, to wit; even by an oath, saying "I live," He desires that credence may be given Him. Oh blessed we, for whose sake God swears! Oh most miserable, if we believe not the Lord even when He swears! What, therefore, God so highly commends, what He even (after human fashion) attests on oath, we are bound of course to approach, and to guard with the utmost seriousness; that, abiding permanently in (the faith of) the solemn pledge of divine grace, we may be able also to persevere in like manner in its fruit and its benefit.

Chapter V.—Sin Never to Be Returned to After Repentance.

For what I say is this, that the repentance which, being shown us and commanded us through God's grace, recalls us to grace with the Lord, when once learned and undertaken by us ought never afterward to be cancelled by repetition of sin. No pretext of ignorance now remains to plead on your behalf; in that, after acknowledging the Lord, and accepting His precepts—in short, after engaging in repentance of (past) sins—you again betake yourself to sins. Thus, in as far as you are removed from ignorance, in so far are you cemented to contumacy. For if the ground on which you had repented of having sinned was that you had begun to fear the Lord, why have you preferred to rescind what you did for fear's sake, except because you have ceased to fear? For there is no other thing but contumacy which subverts fear. Since there is no exception which defends from liability to penalty even such as are ignorant of the Lord—because ignorance of God, openly as He is set before men, and comprehensible as He is even on the score of His heavenly benefits, is not possible—how perilous is it for Him to be despised when known? Now, that man does despise Him, who, after attaining by His help to an understanding of things good and evil, often an affront to his own understanding—that is, to God's gift—by resuming what he understands ought to be shunned, and what he has already shunned: he rejects the Giver in abandoning the gift; he denies the Benefactor in not honoring the benefit. How can he be pleasing to Him, whose gift is displeasing to himself? Thus he is shown to be not only contumacious toward the Lord, but likewise ungrateful. Besides, that man commits no light sin against the Lord, who, after he had by repentance renounced His rival the devil, and had under this appellation subjected him to the Lord, again upraises him by his own return (to the enemy), and makes himself a ground of exultation to him; so that the Evil One, with his prey recovered, rejoices anew against the Lord. Does he not—what is perilous even to say, but must be put forward with a view to edification—place the devil before the Lord? For he seems to have made the comparison who has known each; and to have judicially pronounced him to be the better whose (servant) he has preferred again to be. Thus he who, through repentance for sins, had begun to make satisfaction to the Lord, will, through another repentance of his repentance, make satisfaction to the devil, and will be the more hateful to God in proportion as he will be the more acceptable to His rival. But some say that "God is satisfied if He be looked up to with the heart and the mind, even if this be not done in outward act, and that thus they sin without damage to their fear and their faith:" that is, that they violate wedlock without damage to their chastity; they mingle poison for their parent without damage to their filial duty! Thus, then, they will themselves withal be thrust down into hell without damage to their pardon, while they sin without damage to their fear! Here is a primary example of perversity: they sin, because they fear! I suppose, if they feared not, they would not sin! Let him, therefore, who would not have God offended not revere Him at all, if fear is the plea for offending. But these dispositions have been wont to sprout from the seed of hypocrites, whose friendship with the devil is indivisible, whose repentance never faithful.

Chapter VI—Baptism Not to Be Presumptuously Received. It Requires Preceding Repentance, Manifested by Amendment of Life.

Whatever, then, our poor ability has attempted to suggest with reference to laying hold of repentance once for all, and perpetually retaining it, does indeed bear upon all who are given up to the Lord, as being all competitors for salvation in earning the favor of God; but is chiefly urgent in the case of those young novices who are only just beginning to bedew their ears with divine discourses, and who, as whelps in yet early infancy, and with eyes not yet perfect, creep about uncertainly, and say indeed that they renounce their former deed, and assume (the profession of) repentance, but neglect to complete it. For the very end of desiring importunes them to desire somewhat of their former deeds; just as fruits, when they are already beginning to turn into the sourness or bitterness of age, do yet still in some part flatter their own loveliness. Moreover, a presumptuous confidence in baptism introduces all kind of vicious delay and tergiversation with regard to repentance; for, feeling sure of undoubted pardon of their sins, men meanwhile steal the intervening time, and make it for themselves into a holiday-time for sinning, rather than a time for learning not to sin. Further, how inconsistent is it to expect pardon of sins (to be granted) to a repentance which they have not fulfilled! This is to hold out your hand for merchandise, but not produce the price. For repentance is the price at which the Lord has determined to award pardon: He proposes the redemption of release from penalty at this compensating exchange of repentance. If, then, sellers first examine the coin with which they make their bargains, to see whether it be cut, or scraped, or adulterated, we believe likewise that the Lord, when about to make us the grant of so costly merchandise, even of eternal life, first institutes a probation of our repentance. "But meanwhile let us defer the reality of our repentance: it will then, I suppose, be clear that we are amended when we are absolved." By no means; (but our amendment should be manifested) while, pardon being in abeyance, there is still a prospect of penalty; while the penitent does not yet merit—so far as merit we can—his liberation; while God is threatening, not while He is forgiving. For what slave, after his position has been changed by reception of freedom, charges himself with his (past) thefts and desertions? What soldier, after his discharge, makes satisfaction for his (former) brands? A sinner is bound to bemoan himself before receiving pardon, because the time of repentance is coincident with that of peril and of fear. Not that I deny that the divine benefit—the putting away of sins, I mean—is in every way sure to such as are on the point of entering the (baptismal) water; but what we have to labor for is, that it may be granted us to attain that blessing. For who will grant to you, a man of so faithless repentance, one single sprinkling of any water whatever? To approach it by stealth, indeed, and to get the minister appointed over this business misled by your asseverations, is easy; but God takes foresight for His own treasure, and suffers not the unworthy to steal a march upon it. What, in fact, does He say? "Nothing hid which shall not be revealed." Draw whatever (veil of) darkness you please over your deeds, "God is light." But some think as if God were under a necessity of bestowing even on the unworthy, what He has engaged (to give); and they turn His liberality into slavery. But if it is of necessity that God grants us the symbol of death, then He does so unwillingly. But who permits a gift to be permanently retained which he has granted unwillingly? For do not many afterward fall out of (grace)? is not this gift taken away from many? These, no doubt, are they who do steal a march upon (the treasure), who, after approaching to the faith of repentance, set up on the sands a house doomed to ruin. Let no one, then, flatter himself on the ground of being assigned to the "recruit-classes" of learners, as if on that account he has a license even now to sin. As soon as you "know the Lord," you should fear Him; as soon as you have gazed on Him, you should reverence Him. But what difference does your "knowing" Him make, while you rest in the same practices as in days bygone, when you knew Him not? What, moreover, is it which distinguishes you from a perfected servant of God? Is there one Christ for the baptized, another for the learners? Have they some different hope or reward? some different dread of judgment? some different necessity for repentance? That baptismal washing is a sealing of faith, which faith is begun and is commended by the faith of repentance. We are not washed in order that we may cease sinning, but because we have ceased, since in heart we have been bathed already. For the first baptism of a learner is this, a perfect fear; thenceforward, in so far as you have understanding of the Lord faith is sound, the conscience having once for all embraced repentance. Otherwise, if it is (only) after the baptismal waters that we cease sinning, it is of necessity, not of free-will, that we put on innocence. Who, then, is pre-eminent in goodness? he who is not allowed, or he whom it displeases, to be evil? he who is bidden, or he whose pleasure it is, to be free from crime? Let us, then, neither keep our hands from theft unless the hardness of bars withstand us, nor refrain our eyes from the concupiscence of fornication unless we be withdrawn by guardians of our persons, if no one who has surrendered himself to the Lord is to cease sinning unless he be bound thereto by baptism. But if any entertain this sentiment, I know not whether he, after baptism, do not feel more sadness to think that he has ceased from sinning, than gladness that he hath escaped from it. And so it is becoming that learners desire baptism, but do not hastily receive it: for he who desires it, honors it; he who hastily receives it, disdains it: in the one appears modesty, in the other arrogance; the former satisfies, the latter neglects it; the former covets to merit it, but the latter promises it to himself as a due return; the former takes, the latter usurps it. Whom would you judge worthier, except one who is more amended? whom more amended, except one who is more timid, and on that account has fulfilled the duty of true repentance? for he has feared to continue still in sin, lest he should not merit the reception of baptism. But the hasty receiver, inasmuch as he promised it himself (as his due), being forsooth secure (of obtaining it), could not fear: thus he fulfilled not repentance either, because he lacked the instrumental agent of repentance, that is, fear. Hasty reception is the portion of irreverence; it inflates the seeker, it despises the Giver. And thus it sometimes deceives, for it promises to itself the gift before it be due; whereby He who is to furnish the gift is ever offended.

Chapter VII—Of Repentance, in the Case of Such as Have Lapsed After Baptism.

So long, Lord Christ, may the blessing of learning or hearing concerning the discipline of repentance be granted to Thy servants, as is likewise behooves them, while learners, not to sin; in other words, may they thereafter know nothing of repentance, and require nothing of it. It is irksome to append mention of a second—nay, in that case, the last—hope; lest, by treating of a remedial repenting yet in reserve, we seem to be pointing to a yet further space for sinning. Far be it that any one so interpret our meaning, as if, because there is an opening for repenting, there were even now, on that account, an opening for sinning; and as if the redundancy of celestial clemency constituted a license for human temerity. Let no one be less good because God is more so, by repeating his sin as often as he is forgiven. Otherwise be sure he will find an end of escaping, when he shall not find one of sinning. We have escaped once: thus far and no farther let us commit ourselves to perils, even if we seem likely to escape a second time. Men in general, after escaping shipwreck, thenceforward declare divorce with ship and sea; and by cherishing the memory of the danger, honor the benefit conferred by God—their deliverance, namely. I praise their fear, I love their reverence; they are unwilling a second time to be a burden to the divine mercy; they fear to seem to trample on the benefit which they have attained; they shun, with a solicitude which at all events is good, to make trial a second time of that which they have once learned to fear. Thus the limit of their temerity is the evidence of their fear.

Moreover, man's fear is an honor to God. But however, that most stubborn foe (of ours) never gives his malice leisure; indeed, he is then most savage when he fully feels that a man is freed from his clutches; he then flames fiercest while he is fast becoming extinguished. Grieve and groan he must of necessity over the fact that, by the grant of pardon, so many works of death in man have been overthrown, so many marks of the condemnation which formerly was his own erased. He grieves that that sinner, (now) Christ's servant, is destined to judge him and his angels. And so he observes, assaults, besieges him, in the hope that he may be able in some way either to strike his eyes with carnal concupiscence, or else to entangle his mind with worldly enticements, or else to subvert his faith by fear of earthly power, or else to wrest him from the sure way by perverse traditions: he is never deficient in stumbling-blocks nor in temptations. These poisons of his, therefore, God foreseeing, although the gate of forgiveness has been shut and fastened up with the bar of baptism, has permitted it still to stand somewhat open. In the vestibule He has stationed the second repentance for opening to such as knock: but now once for all, because now for the second time; but never more because the last time it had been in vain. For is not even this once enough? You have what you now deserved not, for you had lost what you had received. If the Lord's indulgence grants you the means of restoring what you had lost, be thankful for the benefit renewed, not to say amplified; for restoring is a greater thing than giving, inasmuch as having lost is more miserable than never having received at all. However, if any do incur the debt of a second repentance, his spirit is not to be forthwith cut down and undermined by despair. Let it by all means be irksome to sin again, but let not to repent again be irksome: irksome to imperil one's self again, but not to be again set free. Let none be ashamed. Repeated sickness must have repeated medicine. You will show your gratitude to the Lord by not refusing what the Lord offers you. You have offended, but can still be reconciled. You have One whom you may satisfy, and Him willing.

Chapter VIII—Examples from Scripture to Prove the Lord's Willingness to Pardon.

This if you doubt, unravel the meaning of "what the Spirit saith to the churches." He imputes to the Ephesians "forsaken love;" reproaches the Thyatirenes with "fornication," and "eating of things sacrificed to idols;" accuses the Sardians of "works not full;" censures the Pergamenes for teaching perverse things; upbraids the Laodiceans for trusting to their riches; and yet gives them all general monitions to repentance—under comminations, it is true; but He would not utter comminations to one unrepentant if He did not forgive the repentant. The matter was doubtful if He had not withal elsewhere demonstrated this profusion of His clemency. Saith He not, “He who hath fallen shall rise again, and he who hath been averted shall be converted?” He it is, indeed, who “would have mercy rather than sacrifices.” The heavens, and the angels who are there, are glad at a man’s repentance. Ho! you sinner, be of good cheer! you see where it is that there is joy at your return. What meaning for us have those themes of the Lord’s parables? Is not the fact that a woman has lost a drachma, and seeks it and finds it, and invites her female friends to share her joy, an example of a restored sinner? There strays, withal, one little ewe of the shepherd’s; but the flock was not more dear than the one: that one is earnestly sought; the one is longed for instead of all; and at length she is found, and is borne back on the shoulders of the shepherd himself; for much had she toiled in straying. That most gentle father, likewise, I will not pass over in silence, who calls his prodigal son home, and willingly receives him repentant after his indigence, slays his best fatted calf, and graces his joy with a banquet. Why not? He had found the son whom he had lost; he had felt him to be all the dearer of whom he had made a gain. Who is that father to be understood by us to be? God, surely: no one is so truly a Father; no one so rich in paternal love. He, then, will receive you, His own son, back, even if you have squandered what you had received from Him, even if you return naked—just because you have returned; and will joy more over your return than over the sobriety of the other; but only if you heartily repent—if you compare your own hunger with the plenty of your Father’s “hired servants”—if you leave behind you the swine, that unclean herd—if you again seek your Father, offended though He be, saying, “I have sinned, nor am worthy any longer to be called Thine.” Confession of sins lightens, as much as dissimulation aggravates them; for confession is counselled by (a desire to make) satisfaction, dissimulation by contumacy.

Chapter IX. —Concerning the Outward Manifestations by Which This Second Repentance is to Be Accompanied.

The narrower, then, the sphere of action of this second and only (remaining) repentance, the more laborious is its probation; in order that it may not be exhibited in the conscience alone, but may likewise be carried out in some (external) act. This act, which is more usually expressed and commonly spoken of under a Greek name, is ἐξομολόγησις , whereby we confess our sins to the Lord, not indeed as if He were ignorant of them, but inasmuch as by confession satisfaction is settled, of confession repentance is born; by repentance God is appeased. And thus exomologesisis a discipline for man's prostration and humiliation, enjoining a demeanor calculated to move mercy. With regard also to the very dress and food, it commands (the penitent) to lie in sackcloth and ashes, to cover his body in mourning, to lay his spirit low in sorrows, to exchange for severe treatment the sins which he has committed; moreover, to know no food and drink but such as is plain,—not for the stomach's sake, to wit, but the soul's; for the most part, however, to feed prayers on fastings, to groan, to weep and make outcries unto the Lord your God; to bow before the feet of the presbyters, and kneel to God's dear ones; to enjoin on all the brethren to be ambassadors to bear his deprecatory supplication (before God). All this exomologesis (does), that it may enhance repentance; may honor God by its fear of the (incurred) danger; may, by itself pronouncing against the sinner, stand in the stead of God's indignation, and by temporal mortification (I will not say frustrate, but) expunge eternal punishments. Therefore, while it abases the man, it raises him; while it covers him with squalor, it renders him more clean; while it accuses, it excuses; while it condemns, it absolves. The less quarter you give yourself, the more (believe me) will God give you.

Chapter X.—Of Men's Shrinking from This Second Repentance and Exomologesis, and of the Unreasonableness of Such Shrinking.

Yet most men either shun this work, as being a public exposure of themselves, or else defer it from day to day. I presume (as being) more mindful of modesty than of salvation; just like men who, having contracted some malady in the more private parts of the body, avoid the privity of physicians, and so perish with their own bashfulness. It is intolerable, forsooth, to modesty to make satisfaction to the offended Lord! to be restored to its forfeited salvation! Truly you are honorable in your modesty; bearing an open forehead for sinning, but an abashed one for deprecating! I give no place to bashfulness when I am a gainer by its loss; when itself in some son exhorts the man, saying, "Respect not me; it is better that I perish through you, i.e. than you through me." At all events, the time when (if ever) its danger is serious, is when it is a butt for jeering speech in the presence of insulters, where one man raises himself on his neighbor's ruin, where there is upward clambering over the prostrate. But among brethren and fellow-servants, where there is common hope, fear, joy, grief, suffering, because there is a common Spirit from a common Lord and Father, why do you think these brothers to be anything other than yourself? Why flee from the partners of your own mischances, as from such as will derisively cheer them? The body cannot feel gladness at the trouble of any one member, it must necessarily join with one consent in the grief, and in laboring for the remedy. In a company of two is the church; but the church is Christ. When, then, you cast yourself at the brethren's knees, you are handling Christ, you are entreating Christ. In like manner, when they shed tears over you, it is Christ who suffers, Christ who prays the Father for mercy. What a son asks is ever easily obtained. Grand indeed is the reward of modesty, which the concealment of our fault promises us! to wit, if we do hide somewhat from the knowledge of man, shall we equally conceal it from God? Are the judgment of men and the knowledge of God so put upon a par? Is it better to be damned in secret than absolved in public? But you say, "It is a miserable thing thus to come to exomologesis:" yes, for evil does bring to misery; but where repentance is to be made, the misery ceases, because it is turned into something salutary. Miserable it is to be cut, and cauterized, and racked with the pungency of some (medicinal) powder: still, the things which heal by unpleasant means do, by the benefit of the cure, excuse their own offensiveness, and make present injury bearable for the sake of the advantage to supervene.

Chapter XI.—Further Strictures on the Same Subject.

What if, besides the shame which they make the most account of, men dread likewise the bodily inconveniences; in that, unwashen, sordidly attired, estranged from gladness, they must spend their time in the roughness of sackcloth, and the horridness of ashes, and the sunkenness of face caused by fasting? Is it then becoming for us to supplicate for our sins in scarlet and purple? Hasten hither with the pin for panning the hair, and the powder for polishing the teeth, and some forked implement of steel or brass for cleaning the nails. Whatever of false brilliance, whatever of feigned redness, is to be had, let him diligently apply it to his lips or cheeks. Let him furthermore seek out baths of more genial temperature in some gardened or seaside retreat; let him enlarge his expenses; let him carefully seek the rarest delicacy of fatted fowls; let him refine his old wine: and when any shall ask him, "On whom are you lavishing all this?" let him say, "I have sinned against God, and am in peril of eternally perishing: and so now I am drooping, and wasting and torturing myself, that I may reconcile God to myself, whom by sinning I have offended." Why, they who go about canvassing for the obtaining of civil office, feel it neither degrading nor irksome to struggle, in behalf of such their desires, with annoyances to soul and body; and not annoyances merely, but likewise contumelies of all kinds. What meannesses of dress do they not affect? what houses do they not beset with early and late visits?—bowing whenever they meet any high personage, frequenting no banquets, associating in no entertainments, but voluntarily exiled from the felicity of freedom and festivity: and all that for the sake of the fleeting joy of a single year! Do we hesitate, when eternity is at stake, to endure what the competitor for consulship or prætorship puts up with? and shall we be tardy in offering to the offended Lord a self-chastisement in food and raiment, which Gentiles lay upon themselves when they have offended no one at all? Such are they of whom Scripture makes mention: "Woe to them who bind their own sins as it were with a long rope."

Chapter XII.—Final Considerations to Induce to Exomologesis.

If you shrink back from exomologesis, consider in your heart the hell, which exomologesis will extinguish for you; and imagine first the magnitude of the penalty, that you may not hesitate about the adoption of the remedy. What do we esteem that treasure-house of eternal fire to be, when small vent-holes of it rouse such blasts of flames that neighboring cities either are already no more, or are in daily expectation of the same fate? The haughtiest mountains start asunder in the birth-throes of their inly-gendered fire; and—which proves to us the perpetuity of the judgment—though they start asunder, though they be devoured, yet come they never to an end. Who will not account these occasional punishments inflicted on the mountains as examples of the judgment which menaces the impenitent? Who will not agree that such sparks are but some few missiles and sportive darts of some inestimably vast center of fire? Therefore, since you know that after the first bulwarks of the Lord's baptism there still remains for you, in exomologesis a second reserve of aid against hell, why do you desert your own salvation? Why are you tardy to approach what you know heals you? Even dumb irrational animals recognize in their time of need the medicines which have been divinely assigned them. The stag, transfixed by the arrow, knows that, to force out the steel, and its inextricable lingerings, he must heal himself with dittany. The swallow, if she blinds her young, knows how to give them eyes again by means of her own swallow-wort. Shall the sinner, knowing that exomologesis has been instituted by the Lord for his restoration, pass that by which restored the Babylonian king to his realms? Long time had he offered to the Lord his repentance, working out his exomologesis by a seven years' squalor, with his nails wildly growing after the eagle's fashion, and his unkempt hair wearing the shagginess of a lion. Hard handling! Him whom men were shuddering at, God was receiving back. But, on the other hand, the Egyptian emperor—who, after pursuing the once afflicted people of God, long denied to their Lord, rushed into the battle—did, after so many warning plagues, perish in the parted sea, (which was permitted to be passable to "the People" alone,) by the backward roll of the waves: for repentance and her handmaid exomologesis he had cast away.

Why should I add more touching these two planks (as it were) of human salvation, caring more for the business of the pen than the duty of my conscience? For, sinner as I am of every dye, and born for nothing save repentance, I cannot easily be silent about that concerning which also the very head and fount of the human race, and of human offence, Adam, restored by exomologesis to his own paradise, is not silent.

Elucidations.

I.

(Such as have lapsed, cap. vii. p. 660.)

The penitential system of the Primitive days, referred to in our author, began to be changed when less public confessions were authorized, on account of the scandals which publicity generated. Changes were as follows:

1. A grave presbyter was appointed to receive and examine voluntary penitents as the Penitentiary of a diocese, and to suspend or reconcile them with due solemnities—circaa.d. 250.

2. This plan also became encumbered with difficulties and was abolished in the East, circaa.d.400.

3. A discipline similar to that of the Anglican Church (which is but loosely maintained therein) succeeded, under St. Chrysostom; who frequently maintains the sufficiency of confession according to Matt. vi. 6. A Gallican author says—"this is the period regarded by historians as the most brilliant in Church history. At the close of the fourth century, in the great churches of the Orient, sixty thousand Christians received the Eucharistic communion, in one day, in both kinds, with no other than their private confessions to Almighty God. The scandalous evil-liver alone was repelled from the Eucharistic Table." This continued till circaa.d.700.

4. Particular, but voluntary confessions were now made in the East and West, but with widely various acceptance under local systems of discipline. The absolutions were precatory: "may God absolve Thee." This lasted, even in the West, till the compulsory system of the Lateran Council, a.d.1215.

5. Since this date, so far as the West is concerned, the whole system of corrupt casuistry and enforced confession adopted in the West has utterly destroyed the Primitive doctrine and discipline as to sin and its remedy wherever it prevails. In the East, private confession exists in a system wholly different and one which maintains the Primitive Theology and the Scriptural principle. (1) It is voluntary; (2) it is free from the corrupt system of the casuists; (3) it distinguishes between Ecclesiastical Absolution and that of Him who alone "seeth in secret;" (4) it admits no compromise with attrition, but exacts the contrite heart and the firm resolve to go and sin no more, and (5) finally, it employs a most guarded and Evangelical formula of remission, of which see Elucidation IV.

II.

(The last hope, cap. vii. p. 662.)

How absolutely the Lateran Council has overthrown the Primitive discipline is here made manifest. The spirit of the latter is expressed by our author in language which almost prompts to despair. It makes sin "exceeding sinful" and even Ecclesiastical forgiveness the reverse of easy. The Lateran System of enforced Confession makes sin easy and restoration to a sinless state equally so: a perpetual resort to the confessor being the only condition for evil living, and a chronic state of pardon and peace. But, let the Greek Church be heard in this matter, rather than an Anglican Catholic. I refer to Macarius, Bishop of Vinnitza and Rector of the Theological Academy of St. Petersburg, as follows: "It is requisite (for the effective reception of Absolution) at least according to the teaching of the Orthodox Church of the Orient, that the following conditions be observed: (1) Contrition for sins, is in the very nature of Penitence, indispensable; (2), consequently, there must be a firm resolution to reform the life; (3) also, faith in Christ and hope in his mercy, with (4) auricular confession before the priest." He allows that this latter condition was not primitive, but was a maternal concession to penitents of later date: this, however, is voluntary, and of a widely different form from that of the Latin, as will appear below in Elucidation IV.

Now, he contrasts with this the system of Rome, and condemns it, on overwhelming considerations. 1. It makes penances compensations or "satisfaction," offered for sins to divine Justice, this (he says) "is in contradiction with the Christian doctrine of justification, the Scripture teaching one full and entire satisfaction for the sins of the whole human race, once for all presented by our Lord Jesus Christ. This doctrine is equally in conflict with the entire teaching of the Primitive Church."

2. It introduces a false system of indulgences, as the consequence of its false premises.

3. He demonstrates the insufficiency of attrition, which respects the fear of punishment, and not sin itself. But the Council of Trent affirms the sufficiency of attrition, and permits the confessor to absolve the attrite. Needless to say, the masses accept this wide gate and broad way to salvation rather than the strait gate and narrow way of hating sin and reforming the life, in obedience to the Gospel.

III.

(Among brethren, cap. x., p. 662.)

A controversial writer has lately complained that Bp. Kaye speaks of the public confession treated of by our author in this work, and adds—"Tertullian nowhere used the word public." The answer is that he speaks of the discipline of Exomologesis, which was, in its own nature, as public as preaching. A Gallican writer, less inclined to Jesuitism in the use of words, says frankly: "When one studies this question, with the documents before his eyes, it is impossible not to confess that the Primitive discipline of the Church exhibits not a vestige of the auricular confession afterwards introduced." See Irenæus, Adv. Hæres. Vol. I. p. 335, this Series. The Lii. of the canons called Apostolical, reflects a very simple view of the matter, in these words: "If any Bishop or Presbyter will not receive one who turns from his sins, but casts him out, let him be deposed: for he grieves Christ, who said, There shall be joy in heaven over one sinner that repenteth." The ascetic spirit of our author seems at war with that of this Canon.

IV.

(Exomologesis, cap. xii., p. 663.)

To this day, in the Oriental Churches, the examination of the presbyter who hears the voluntary confession of penitents, is often very primitive in its forms and confined to general inquiries under the Decalogue. The Casuistry of (Dens and Liguori) the Western Schemata Practica has not defiled our Eastern brethren to any great extent.

In the office (᾿Ακολουθία τῶν ἐξομολουγουμένων) we have a simple and beautiful form of prayer and supplication in which the following is the formula of Absolution: "My Spiritual child, who hast confessed to my humility, I, unworthy and a sinner, have not the power to forgive sins on Earth; God only can: and through that Divine voice which came to the Apostles, after the Resurrection of our Lord Jesus Christ, saying—'Whosoever sins, etc.,' we, therein confiding, say—Whatsoever thou hast confessed to my extreme humility, and whatsoever thou hast omitted to say, either through ignorance or forgetfulness, God forgive thee in this present world and in that which is to come."

The plural (Wethere in confiding) is significant and a token of Primitive doctrine: i.e. of confession before the whole Church, (2 Cor. ii. 10): and note the precatory form— "God forgive thee." The perilous form Ego te absolve is not Catholic: it dates from the thirteenth century and is used in the West only. It is not wholly dropped from the Anglican Office, but has been omitted from the American Prayer-Book.

www.ingramcontent.com/pod-product-compliance
Lightning Source LLC
Chambersburg PA
CBHW071015120726
47910CB00004B/1526

* 9 7 8 1 6 4 3 7 3 0 8 9 9 *